KING ARTHUR

RICHARD BRASSEY

Orion
Children's Books

First published in Great Britain in 2012
by Orion Children's Books
a division of the Orion Publishing Group Ltd
Orion House, 5 Upper St Martin's Lane, London WC2H 9EA
An Hachette UK Company

10 9 8 7 6 5 4 3 2 1

A catalogue record for this book is available from the British Library

Printed in China

ISBN 978 1 4440 0128 0

www.orionbooks.co.uk

HOW MIGHT ARTHUR'S KNIGHTS HAVE LOOKED?

King Arthur is famous for his Knights of
the Round Table. We cannot say exactly
how they looked. Perhaps they wore a
mix of what we know Roman soldiers and
Saxon warriors wore at the time.

WHO WAS KING ARTHUR?

Nearly all agree that, if King Arthur was indeed a real person, he must have lived in the time after the Romans left Britain. But who was he ...

A British warlord, out for all he could grab in a land without order?

A Roman officer, who stayed to defend Britannia from the Saxons?

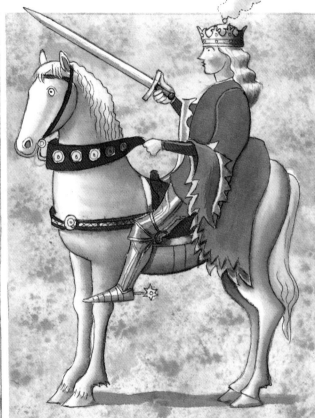

A faerie king who will one day return to rescue his people from danger?

Or does the mystery surrounding Arthur mean you can imagine him to be whoever you wish?

Around 407 A.D. the Romans left Britain never to return. Their fine walled cities, their palaces and temples, villas, farms, vineyards, fields of wheat and long straight roads ... all lay at the mercy of the fierce Saxons in their longboats.

THE PAX ROMANA
A long period when most people living in the Roman Empire enjoyed peace and freedom from war.

Our villa boasts central heating and mosaic floors.

Roman leaders fought with each other to be Emperor. One of these was Constantine III, the last Roman general to leave Britain. Legend tells us that Constantine had a son, named Uther Pendragon, who became King of Britain after his father's death.

We are told that Uther loved Igraine, the wife of the Duke of Cornwall. For this reason the Duke kept Igraine safe in his castle of Tintagel.

One night the magician, Merlin, changed Uther's shape into that of the Duke. In this guise Uther entered Tintagel unchallenged. That same night the Duke was killed by Uther's men in battle.

Then Uther made Igraine his wife and they had a son. His name was Arthur.

Soon after Arthur's birth, Uther gave him to Merlin who took him away to live with a knight named Sir Ector. Arthur grew up never knowing he was Uther's son.

TINTAGEL

Archaeological finds mean we know for sure that Tintagel was a Roman stronghold, and probably the HQ of a British king after they left. Jars which held olive oil and wine show trade with Europe continued, as did the Roman way of life.

When Uther died his sword appeared fixed by magic in an anvil. On the blade were these words: "Whoso pulleth out this sword from this stone is the true king of all England". All the lords of the kingdom tried and all failed.

Do it again!

We will hav Arthur for our King!

Then, by chance, Arthur had a go. The sword came out easily. All agreed he should be king. Merlin became his advisor and told him the truth of his birth.

MIXED-UP MERLIN

Writers who collected stories about Arthur often got muddled. Merlin was probably a mix-up of two legendary characters: *Myrrdin* and *Emrys* became *Merlin Ambrosius*. But he's such a good character that Arthur's story wouldn't be the same without him.

There are two fighting dragons trapped in the hill underneath!

In Welsh myth, Emrys was a boy with magic powers who told an ancient king, Vortigern, the reason his castle kept falling down.

Myrrdin may have been a real man from Northern Britain, who lived in the forest with wild animals and was said to be able to see into the future.

EXCALIBUR

Arthur fought many battles after he became king. In one he broke his sword. Merlin led him to a lake, from the middle of which reached an arm holding the magical sword Excalibur. Here they met the Lady of the Lake who gave Excalibur to Arthur.

CAMELOT

Arthur is said to have held court in a magnificent palace called Camelot.

It was at Camelot that he married Guinevere, the daughter of King Leodegrance, whose wedding present to him was the famous Round Table. Here Arthur feasted with his knights and all were equal, since a round table has no head. During the wedding a white hart raced into the hall pursued by a hound.

Nobody can say exactly where Camelot might have been. Some say Tintagel. Some say ancient Cadbury Castle in Somerset, atop a huge manmade hill which you can still see today.

My name is Alfred the Great. I'm the king who burnt the cakes!

Some say Winchester because they muddle Arthur's name with the later King Alfred, who definitely existed and whose capital was at Winchester.

I'm just as great a king as he ever was.

At Winchester Castle there's a round table. King Henry VIII was so sure it was the real thing that he had a picture of himself as King Arthur painted on it. But we now know the table was made long after Arthur's time.

MORGAN LE FAY

Arthur had an older half-sister, the daughter of his mother, Igraine, and the Duke of Cornwall. Morgan Le Fay had magic powers and lived on the mysterious Isle of Avalon. Some say she was jealous of Arthur and plotted against him.

THE KNIGHTS OF THE ROUND TABLE

Over the centuries, with each new telling of Arthur's story, more knights were added from other legends and other stories.

TRISTRAM
a Cornish knight who fell in love with his aunt

LANCELOT DU LAC
who fell in love with Guinevere

PERCEVAL
a Grail knight

GALAHAD
who sat in the chair of a perfect knight

KAY
Arthur's half-brother

MORDRED
Arthur's nephew who betrayed him

From Camelot they set out on their adventures to battle knights, giants and dragons, to rescue damsels and to overcome magic.

GAWAIN
who fought a dragon

PALOMIDES
a Saracen who pursued
the questing beast

Before the Romans left, Christianity had arrived in Britain. Arthur is often seen as a Christian champion who held out against the invading Saxons and their pagan gods. There are also many stories of a holy relic, the Grail, which was stolen from Arthur's court. After this theft a lot of his knights' time was spent trying to find it again.

THE HOLY GRAIL

A story was told that Joseph, who had carried Jesus to his tomb after the crucifixion, caught some of Jesus's blood in a cup, known as a grail. Joseph had then carried this to the Isle of Avalon in England.

THE ISLE OF AVALON?

In 1191 the monks of Glastonbury Abbey announced that they'd found the graves of Arthur and Guinevere. Ever since, Glastonbury has been closely linked to Arthur. The unusual hill of Glastonbury Tor was once surrounded by water and is often claimed to be Avalon - the magical Island of Apples.

Guess what? I think we may have found King Arthur's bones!

THE GLASTONBURY THORN

When Joseph came to Avalon he stuck his staff in the ground. Here it sprouted into a thorn tree, which unusually flowered twice a year. It is said that a descendant of this tree still grows in the grounds of Glastonbury Abbey.

Sir Galahad eventually found the Grail and went up to heaven with it. Meanwhile Arthur's other knights had grown old and tired in the quest. Mordred was jealous of his uncle Arthur. He told him that Guinevere was in love with Lancelot.

Arthur sentenced Guinevere to death as a traitor but Lancelot rescued her. While this argument was going on, Mordred stole the throne. Arthur was forced to fight him at the battle of Camlann. Arthur killed Mordred but was fatally wounded himself.

The wounded Arthur told Sir Bedevere to carry him to a lake and throw Excalibur into it. A hand reached from the water and caught the sword. Then a boat appeared bearing four queens, including Morgan Le Fay and the Lady of the Lake. They took Arthur away to the Isle of Avalon to heal his wounds and he was never seen again.

LE MORTE D'ARTHUR

For centuries after the Romans left hardly anybody wrote history. What books there were had to be hand-copied by monks, who often got muddled or made up stories ... especially exciting stories about a hero called Arthur.

Then in 1485, a thousand years after Arthur might have been, William Caxton, owner of the first printing press in England, published *Le Morte d'Arthur* by Sir Thomas Malory. This collected and confused nearly all the stories we now associate with King Arthur into one book. It was a huge bestseller.

At Builth Wells in Wales there is said to be a paw print left by Arthur's hound, Cabal.

Arthur is said to have been buried under mountains as far apart as Etna in Sicily and Arthur's Seat in Edinburgh.

Uther is said to be buried under Stonehenge, though it was built thousands of years before he might have lived.

The first Arthurian-style tournament was in Cyprus in 1223. People still dress up and hold such events today.

THE HARRY POTTER OF THE MIDDLE AGES

During the Crusades, British and French knights carried stories of Arthur all over Europe and the Middle East. King Arthur became as popular as Harry Potter is today. More and more characters and tall tales kept being added to Arthur's story.

The Victorians went nuts for everything Arthurian. They dressed up as knights and held pageants in all weathers. The prime minister, Disraeli, even led a move to restore Arthurian chivalry to England.

Prince Albert and Queen Victoria were painted as Arthur and Guinevere. The poet laureate, Tennyson, wrote long Arthurian poems which were bestsellers. T Queen liked them so much she made him a baron.

In the 20th century lots of books were written about Arthur. *The Sword in the Stone* became a Disney film.

From *Don Quixote* to *Star Wars*, books, plays, operas, films, television series and computer games have all been influenced by Arthurian legend.

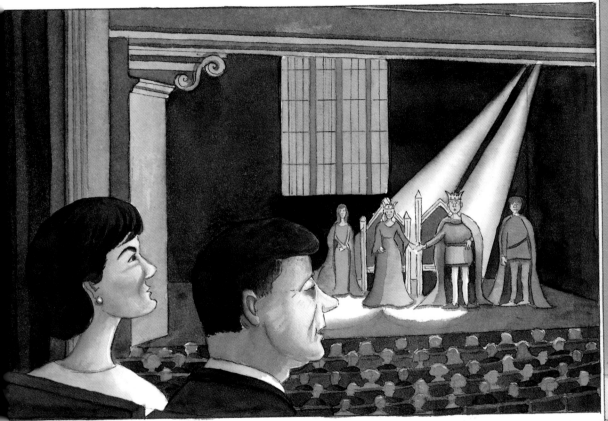

In 1960, just after he was elected US President, John F. Kennedy and his wife Jackie attended the first night of the musical *Camelot*. During his short and hopeful presidency, the White House became known as Camelot.

More than ever before appear every year.

MERLIN'S FATE

Legend tells us Merlin took an apprentice, named Nimuë, who cast a spell which trapped him in a tree. Here Merlin awaits the return of Arthur.

Mystery still surrounds the death of Arthur. It is said that on his grave were these words ...

HERE LIES ARTHUR, THE ONCE AND FUTURE KING

Did Arthur really exist? Is he only sleeping until his countr most needs him in the future. Whatever the truth, no one can deny how his legend lives on. In the words of the famous British Prime Ministe Winston Churchill ...

It is all true ... or it ought to be!